The Art of Prediction

Anticipate, Calculate and Out-Strategize Your Competitors

By Richard Carey

Copyright 2017 by Richard Carey

Published by Make Profits Easy LLC

Profitsdaily123@aol.com

facebook.com/MakeProfitsEasy

Table of Contents

Introduction 4

Chapter 1: Assess Your Situation – Formulate Your Plan Win with an Effective Defense 8

Chapter 2: Win with a Strategic Offense 17

Chapter 3: Recognize Opportunities Before Your Competition Does 30

Chapter 4: What if ...You Could Create Opportunities? 36

Chapter 5: Know Your Customer 43

Chapter 6: Using Social Media to Outsmart Your Competition..47

Chapter 7: Use Guerilla Fighting Tactics to Outsmart Your Competition 56

Chapter 8: Learn To Trust Your Instincts...................61

Chapter 9: Find Your Niche Market 66

Chapter 10: How To Negotiate And Seal The Deal ... 73

Chapter 11: Be The Leader Who Comes Out Ahead .. 78

Conclusion 83

Introduction

Do you dread or welcome competition? Competition has a dual reputation. On the one hand, we all understand that a company, idea or person thrives when there is competition. Imagine being stranded on an island and running every day for exercise. It's fun, you get faster as you go, but what standards do you use to measure excellence and progress? In an important way, competition defines us.

Without competition, we have no reason to strive to be the best. That applies to business, as well. Are you cursing your competitor for undercutting you and making you struggle for customers?

You should be rejoicing instead. It's that competitor that is nudging you forward, bringing out the best in you to help you succeed.

Whether you're number 1 or number 2, everyone gains from competition. And this book will help you grab the number 1 spot. It will show you how to act in ways that enable you to be your best as you outthink and outsmart the competition. You're getting to know him or her and will be able to predict his or her action or response; and you'll be prepared.

The fact is, if you don't have competition, you probably don't have an idea or product that anyone will be interested in for longer than a month. Therefore, whether you are leading or following the competition, be grateful that you have a rival breathing down your neck. Having competitors is a visible validation that you are doing something right. Don't ever fear your competition. Learn from them, and do what they do better. Recognize their value to the market and make it your mission to get ahead and crush them. We'll discover how to surpass and outsmart your competition in the following chapters.

Many of us equate competition with dog-eat-dog capitalistic warfare. Nothing could be further from the truth. The definitive scripture on how to win over your competition was written in 5th century China based on the legendary Master Sun Tzu. While the ideas deal with war, the applications are more far-reaching. Instead of doing battle, The Art of War discussed how to outsmart and outwit the enemy. Many businesses, entrepreneurs and athletes have found winning inspiration in its wisdom.

Studies have shown that natural leaders and entrepreneurs have a very specific mindset. Instead of using linear thinking that reacts to situations and the environment, entrepreneurial thinking is a proactive belief that an individual creates and controls his or her own circumstances and environment. With this mindset, you control what happens instead of being controlled by the government, economy or other influences. Entrepreneurs act instead of reacting. They don't wait for events to change, they create the events most favorable to their ultimate success.

Entrepreneurs and leaders are in control of their circumstances, which allows them to work toward and predict the outcome. Outsmarting their competitors is not a matter of gazing into a looking glass. It's a matter of creating the circumstances that will make those prediction a reality. And because they take control, they will persevere until their goals are achieved.

It doesn't matter what business you are in. The more you take control of your environment, the more you will be able to predict the outcome.

Doing business is a battle. This book will prepare you with the mindset, ideas and strategies you need to outsmart, outwit your competition and win.

Chapter 1: Assess Your Situation – Formulate Your Plan Win with an Effective Defense

> It is a matter of life and death, a road either to safety or to ruin. – Sun Tzu

If you're in business, you want to develop and increase your market share. It's that simple. If someone else is offering the product or services you are, you need a demonstrable reason why customers should choose you. In order for that to happen, you need to assess the marketplace, as well as your competition. Because your competitor will be after the same customers. In order to come out ahead, you need to be able to predict what your competitor will do and outsmart and outwit him.

Before you even think about your customers, you need to assess your competition. Information is power, and the more data you can gather, the more options you have. This means: know what your competition is planning or will plan when you make your move. This seems very basic, yet a 2005 study showed that less than ten percent of business managers do so.

One reason for this dissonance is that the majority of managers spend most of their time focusing on *their* product or service – when do we launch, what is the cost, who is our customer? They are focused inwardly. To predict how your competitor will react, you must shift your focus outward. If you don't know how your competition will react to your next move, you might be in for an unpleasant surprise.

You need to keep in mind your competitor has choices in how to react, and those choices could harm or benefit you. Can you afford not to spend time evaluating your competitor in greater detail? The truth is, this is rarely done. And when it is, it can make the different between success and failure.

Predicting your competitor's responses is a value tool that many executives fail to use. How well do you understand your competition? Can he or she afford a financial risk? What are their resources? Different answers will require different tactics on your part. Consider having knowledge about your competitor an asset that doesn't show up on the balance sheet, but is equally as important as the numbers.

Equally relevant to any decision you make are the competitor's individual decision makers. This goes beyond crunching numbers (companies love doing that) and moves you into the realm of gathering important insight into your competitor to help you plan *your* move. You always want to remain in control. In today's information-driven world, getting this type of data is easy. And the insight gathered can prove invaluable. Luckily for you, too many companies fail to it.

While you are strategizing on behalf of your own business, strategize your competitor's response. Those are the weapons top generals, top business executives and smart entrepreneurs use. Your competitor's response to your plan is limited by its own resources, so the more you know, the more accurately you can predict his move. Business can be a challenging chess game, and you want to think several steps ahead of your competition.

In war, you want to avoid unpleasant surprises. The proper research will provide clues as to how your competitor is likely to act, so that you can be prepared.

The information you should have is: the competitor's assets that are tangible and not so tangible, such as brand recognition, goodwill, knowledge, talent and market position.

When you make plans for your company, see it from your competitor's point of view, which is especially helpful when you know who those decision-makers are. Top executives usually make branding and corporate financial decision, while sales executive frequently determine the individual pricing of a product or service. Other factors, such as unions and international local customs and habits also need to be considered.

This is a lot of information to gather, but having it will help you predict your competitions moves and will put you in at greater advantage than the average company owner or thinker. And in business, you want every advantage you can get.

All this effort will certainly pay off, but in business, as in life, you need to be prepared for the unexpected. Perhaps some of your data is incomplete, faulty, or simply out-of-date. Perhaps you've misjudged the decision makers, or maybe the company simply will react in unexpected ways. Consider this a learning experience. Determine what went wrong, what vital data did you miss or misinterpret, and what enabled the competitor to act against expectations? Making this a continuing, ongoing effort in your planning strategy will minimize errors and maximize your ability to have accurate and usable information at your fingertips. This will result in fewer miscalculations and greater opportunities for you to lead the market in your field.

Thanks to modern technology, keeping an eye on your competition is easy than it ever was. Facebook and Twitter are a fount of valuable information. It's amazing what people and companies will broadcast to the world. Customer reviews are another good way to track a company's strengths and shortcoming. Sign up for any newsletter the company may regularly send out. That's one way of finding out about new or updated products.

One of the most overlooked source of information are your own customers. Simply ask new customers whom they dealt with previously and why did they stop. You'd be surprised what you might find out. Sooner or later, a clearer picture of your competition should emerge.

Every industry has its trade shows. Yet, very few companies visit their competitor's booths for literature and information. Outsmart your competition by sending one of your employees for any available brochures, samples and conversation with the person manning the booth.

Hiring a competitor's former employee can give you inside information as to where the competitor is headed and what problems the company is or will be facing. No one will be more eager to chat than a disgruntled ex-employee, and you shouldn't hesitate to use such a valuable asset. On the flip side, keep an eye on who the competitor is hiring. Job descriptions tend to be fairly specific. If they are looking for certain technology skills, it might give you a hint about their future plans. If they are consistently hiring many people, it could indicate a rapid turnover in personnel and internal problems. Sometimes, it doesn't take a Sherlock Holmes to establish a picture.

All this information gathering may seem labor intensive. But you'll be amazed what you can deduce from just a few facts. To outsmart your competition, you need the extra edge that information can provide.

> *If you know the enemy and know yourself, you need not fear the result of a hundred battles. If you know yourself but not the enemy, for every victory gained you will also suffer a defeat. If you know neither the enemy nor yourself, you will succumb in every battle.* – Sun Tzu

As a general, or business leader, you must have a plan long before you start to act. Know who you are up against. And know yourself and your team. Communicate with your team. Consider your team your most important asset. Many companies and entrepreneurs today outsource needed services to remain more cost effective. While outsourcing can save money, it may not always be in your best interest to do so when you are preparing to overtake your competitor. When you outsource a part of your valuable team, you risk losing control. Someone else is managing a part of your overall strategy and plan. And it may not be as cost-effective as it seems when you add in legal fees to review contracts between you and the outsourced party.

Most importantly, the outsourcing party won't be driven with the same passion and motives that are driving you. Their ultimate goals will not be your goals.

Therefore, when you assemble your team to take on the opposition, create a team with your vision and standards. And keep them close.

Chapter 2: Win with a Strategic Offense

> "When the enemy is relaxed, make them toil. When full, starve them. When settled, make them move." – Sun Tzu

We have discussed what can be described as defensive strategies. You study, plan and become prepared. That should be your first step in besting your competitor. There are times, however, when offensive moves are necessary and advisable to defeat your competition. Both you and your competitor are likely to be after the same customers. At the same time, you want to acquire some of your competitor's existing customers and market share. If you want to win this fight, you need a better offense. You must be able to convince customers how and why you have more to offer than your competitor. You need a pro-active, offensive strategy.

The logical way to begin your offense is with the planning strategies outlined in Chapter 1. Specifically, you need to know your competitor's weaknesses and how to exploit them. By outsmarting your competitor with a full-frontal attack, you are in a position to place your product in a leadership position. This is not being rude. It means you are stronger, better and have more to offer. That is the essence of succeeding in business. Through extensive advertising and the use of all of your resources, you will introduce your service or product in ways that will inspire customers to shift their allegiance from your competitor to you. In war, as in business, this is called divide and conquer. When handled strategically, an entrepreneur or small business can challenge a long-time business Goliath and come out ahead.

Going on the offense in business is like engaging your competitor in a game of chess. The battle is up front, in full view. Instead of planning a quiet defense in the background, all acts are out there and exposed. The two generals – or CEOs – are locked in eye contact in a game where every move counts. Your day-to-day movements are the men shifting across the board. Every move you make should weaken your competitor's position and strengthen yours. The only thing not showing is your ultimate master business plan. It is this plan that will ultimately be used to defeat your opponent's weakness.

A perfect example of a David-like company taking on and winning against established, large and popular Goliath competitors is Harley Davidson. While Japanese motorcycles ruled the global market, Harley Davidson was driven close to bankruptcy by the Japanese imports that customers wanted. In the 1980s, Harley Davidson suffered from a severe quality and customer satisfaction decline. Nearly bankrupt, they probably weren't even on Japan's marketing radar. And that was a serious mistake. Remember the lesson in Chapter 1. Always know what your competition is doing; always have a plan to deal with him or her.

Harley-Davidson made some radical changes to which no one was paying attention. They lobbied for increased tariffs on the import of motorcycles from Japan. Then, they overhauled their quality-control department and improved the design and quality of their motorcycles. To add insult to injury, they instituted an excellent Japanese-style management program that broaden the decision-making ability of middle management. They clearly had a superior offensive strategy relative their Japanese competition, who wasn't paying attention and remained oblivious to what was happening. Then, they took it a step further. Harley Davidson created a social brand before there was such a thing as branding. They marketed their motorcycles as a lifestyle choice, safe enough for the 1980s, but wild enough for those with illusion of rebellion.

Within a year, H-D's sales were increasing, and they soon dominated the American market, making Japanese imports inconsequential. A struggling company facing financial disaster bested and outmaneuvered the almost unbeatable Japanese competition that had a firm grip on the world market.

Harley Davidson started with a problem, created a well-developed plan, then gave its customers a product that would fuel dreams of socially acceptable rebellion, which created tremendous and instant customer loyalty. By the 1990s, they were dominating Japan's own market for heavy-class motorcycles.

When a company wants a greater market share, offensive marketing is one of the most valuable tools to outwit the competition. While we have discussed that it is accepted strategy to use a competitor's weakness against him, it is also necessary to be prepared for the competitor's response. Therefore, the company should be very clear as to the reason it deserves customer consideration. It needs to take active control and convince potential customers that:

1. Our product is of higher quality than our competitor's.
2. Our company is community-related and socially conscious while our competition is impersonally global.
3. Our company provides more than our competition.
4. Our product will help you while our competitor's product won't.

These offensive strategies are effective on customer's who are already dealing with the competition but find the arguments persuasive, or customers who haven't yet decided which company to use. If used effectively, they can garner you a larger market share by predicting and addressing what the customer wants to hear. The best way is to have done the research and planning described in Chapter 1 by locating the competition's vulnerable areas. By maximizing the competitor's weaknesses and minimizing their strengths, you can effectively outsmart your competitor by seizing a portion of the available market share.

For example, imagine two stores selling the same type of dresses. One store loudly advertises its affordable low prices. Could the second store lure customers by also promising a bargain? No, because the promises would cancel each other out. To outsmart the first store, the second store should loudly proclaim its high quality and elegant styles. It needs to set itself apart from the first store. By doing this, the second store will lure customers who prefer style over a good price.

Another effective offensive way to outsmart the competition is not just to hit them when they are down, but to sell the customer a fantasy. Perfume advertising does that very effectively by implying that wearing a certain fragrance will change your life. The problem is that all perfume companies use the same strategy, preventing any one from standing out. When you are doing exactly what your competition is doing, it doesn't matter how good you are, it's difficult to gain market share.

Addressing a potential customer's fantasy can be done very effectively, however, if it is done uniquely and unexpectedly. An example of this are the 1980's ads for the now-defunct New York Helmsley hotel. All hotels ads promise the best rooms at the best rates. There is nothing unique or unexpected. The Helmsley ads depicted the glamorous owner, Leona Helmsley, insisting that she would only accept the very finest – no skimpy sheets or towels for her. "I won't settle. Why should you?" She wasn't selling hotel rooms. Mrs. Helmsley was selling glamour. And the emotional appeal worked. The hotel's occupancy rate almost quadrupled. In order to outwit your competitor, you must not only know him or her, but you must understand your customer, as well. You must answer a need. We will be discussing this further in this book.

Using an offensive strategy is most effective if you are not the leader, but you promise to offer something that the leader does not have. Remember Avis' "We're Number 2, And We Try Harder" campaign? They stated flat-out that their competition, Hertz, had a greater market share. But their ad implied more attentiveness and better customer service. They were going to work harder for their customers. The company also positioned itself as the lovable underdog everyone could relate to. The campaign was an immediate success as the market share between Avis and Hertz narrowed significantly.

If you want to outsmart your competition, you need to offer customers something your competitor does not. When given the option, you want the customer to choose *you,* so give him or her a good reason to reject the other guy.

A dry cleaner or clothing boutique can offer extra services, such as tailoring or delivery. If you own a furniture store, start a decorating blog or provide decorating advice online. A supermarket can provide online or in-store recipes. People notice these little touches and appreciate them.

Provide something of value as a bonus, and you will be depleting your competitor's customer base.

Service tends to be more of an issue with many consumers than price, so don't be afraid to make your services a little more expensive when you have real value to offer. Sometimes, a cheap price can be interpreted as low-quality products or service.

Another way to actively meet a customer's need is to be able to be available. No company answers their phones these days, thereby forcing customers to go through a long push-button option game. Everyone feels that particular frustration. Something as simple as being easy to reach on the phone can be a tremendous asset to your company.

An important offensive marketing strategy is to create your own brand. Branding is about breaking your product through all the other choices and making it more desirable. Branding is image more than product. Take the sneaker industry. There is an avalanche of choices, but certain brands have become "cool." Are they necessarily better and more functional? No, they aren't. But their branding makes the wearer "cool." Sneakers used to be simple gym shoes. Then Nike, along with Michael Jordan, made them a status symbol. Everyone wanted a pair, or, more accurately, *needed* a pair. Not having a pair of Jordan's was a social black mark, especially among the trendy teenage set. Buyers didn't care about how well the sneaker was made, they wanted to be seen wearing a specific brand of sneaker. A strong brand can raise your product into the stratosphere. Branding goes beyond advertising; it's all about the image that it leaves in the mind of the consumer. A brand is a promise to the buyer. Nike promises that wearing its sneakers will make you special. Pay attention to perfume ads. They rarely talk about the actual scent, or the actual product. They create an image and a promise of a once-in-a-lifetime romantic adventure. It's an emotional appeal that works.

When creating your brand, imagine what your customer really wants – a cool image or a hot romance. By predicting your customer's needs and wants and fulfilling them, you will outsmart your competitor, who is merely offering a product.

In 2009, when we experienced the worst economic conditions since the Great Depression, companies were down-sizing or closing. People were losing jobs. Businesses were suffering through record loses. So how did Apple enjoy one of the most profitable years it ever had? Three reasons contributed to their success. Steve Job never gave up. He believed in his products, which were the best on the market, and yes, the most expensive. As we will see, price isn't the only factor when people make buying decisions. The third, and most important reason for Apple's success was its branding. People *had* to have their products. Does anyone really need an iPhone that costs $1,000? No, but Apple's branding has positioned its products so that people will do anything to have them, regardless of the cost. Like the Jordan sneakers, they successfully created a need and an image that without their product, the consumer is lacking something important.

Do not underestimate the power of branding.

Chapter 3: Recognize Opportunities Before Your Competition Does

Opportunities multiply as they are seized. – Sun Tzu

Opportunity is missed by most people because it is dressed in overalls and looks like work. - Thomas Edison

You not only want to predict the outcome of a struggle between you and your competitor, you want to succeed. You are in the game to win. Some people, usually those who do *not* come out ahead, believe it comes down to luck. That belief is why these strugglers will never outsmart their competition. To paraphrase Tina Turner, "What's Luck Got To Do With It?"

To win, you need to seize all opportunities before your competition does. These opportunities are there, all around us, like hidden gems. When you consciously and consistently reach for opportunities, they become part of your strategic planning. The question is, how do you uncover these opportunities before your competitor does? The answer is, always be prepared and working toward your goal.

You've been spending time analyzing your competition. That's a crucial step in predicting his or her actions. Now, it's time to take it a step further.

Start paying attention to the small, upstart companies in your field. They may just be starting out and not a threat to your business, but they may be using new ideas and technology. The reason they started their business may be to implement something new. Outsmart your main competitors by watching the upstarts.

Don't be predictable. There's a high probability your competition is watching you, just as you are watching them. Outsmart them by not revealing your every move. This is another reason keeping staff in-house rather than outsourcing can help you outwit the competition. In-house gives you greater control about what information is released and what is kept from the public.

Use customer feedback as a major learning opportunity. Many companies provide the opportunity for feedback, but how many actually use the information to improve service? Very few, and the odds are, your competitor isn't. He or she may not know how to engage or work with customers so as to get them to come back. The lack of satisfactory customer service is one of the biggest consumer complaints. If you stand apart from the rest and use customer feedback as a means to improve your product and service, you will be drawing a huge share of the market to your side.

Actively look for opportunities instead of passively waiting. Opportunity usually doesn't politely knock at the door. Sometimes, you need to grab it and drag it in. Keep an open mind when it comes to "business as usual." We all find comfort in the familiar. You're used to doing things a certain way, and it works. Logically, you conclude that any other way won't work. Accept the possibility of approaching your business in a different way. Opportunity requires stepping outside your comfort zone. As smart as you are in running your business, you might not know everything. Be open to new methods of solving problems to help you move ahead of your competitor, who likely is handling problems the same way they have always been handled.

Technology and access to new knowledge are changing the business world as we know it. What worked for you last month may not be the best way today. Look for opportunities to improve on tried-and-true methods instead of getting locked in a mental box.

Remember how exciting it was to be able to rent movies from Blockbuster? You drove to the local outlet and rented your favorite flicks over the weekend. It worked beautifully, and everyone loved it. Blockbuster happily rested on its laurels. Then came Netflix with the idea of streaming movies online, without you having to leave the comfort of your sofa. As a result, Blockbusters is out of business, and Netflix is thriving.

Opportunities come when you pay attention and watch for them. Uber started as a taxi delivery service and is quite successful. Did it stop there? No, Uber paid attention to what people needed. Undoubtedly, many of them were its own customers, who called Uber to be driven to a restaurant in order to pick up food. This is how UberEATS was born. UberEATS now picks up and delivers food straight your door. They even deliver from McDonald's. Delivery from a fast-food company used to be inconceivable. But by merely paying attention, Uber created a whole new business venture.

Pay attention to your customer's needs, especially if you've been in business for a while and are becoming comfortable. Is your company answering the needs of an ever-growing immigrant population? Are you using Facebook, Twitter and other social network to showcase your business and communicate with potential customers? Do you have an engaging blog that provides interesting information?

Do you listen to your staff when someone says, "If we could do it this way ....?" Many people are locked in the mindset that if it ain't broke, don't fix it. It's a bad mindset for creating new opportunities and innovations. Listen to ideas from you staff when they are offered. *"Treat your men as you would your sons." – Sun Tzu.*

While you are analyzing your competition (See Chapter 1), be honest about what they are doing right. Learn and do it better.

Chapter 4: What if ...You Could Create Opportunities?

> "A pessimist sees the difficulty in every opportunity; an optimist sees the opportunity in every difficulty." Winston S. Churchill

If you have unique ideas, you can predict that your competitor probably won't be thinking along the same lines. That is why being creative is an important element in outsmarting him or her. We have discussed the importance of looking for opportunities. To win in business and outthink your competitor, you also have to be prepared to *create* opportunities. This is being proactive rather than reactive.

An opportunity is a need that can be filled. If you are able to do that, customers will be knocking at your door. But what if there is no immediate need? What if, on the surface, everything is fine and taken care of?

That's when you create a need that no one knew existed. The best recent example of that is Uber. Uber provides transportation from point A to point B. Buses, cars and taxis have handled that problem for over a hundred years. What did two young men do in 2008 that resulted in a $50 billion company by 2014 and continues to thrive today, cutting a huge chunk out of the Goliath taxi cab business?

Travis Kalanick and Garrett Camp were two Americans visiting Paris. On a grim, rainy night, they stuck out their arms by a curb, hoping for a cab to come along. Luck failed them, and grumpily, they returned to their hotel. When they returned home to San Francisco, they experienced the same vexing problem. Cabs fill a great need, but you can't always get one when you need one.

They were tech-savvy people, and out of their vexation grew an idea. Apps were becoming very popular at the time, and they created an app that allowed you to get a cab within minutes by simply pushing a button.

The men of Uber made everyone aware of the problems that could arise with taxicabs and *created* a solution as well as a need. Their competition, the taxi cab companies, publicly helped Uber by loudly complaining about this interloper cutting into their business. Remember the rule in Chapter 2 that says to emphasize your own strength and your competitor's weakness? The cab companies did the exact opposite and paid the price. With their loud complaints, they drew attention to *their own* weakness and Uber's *strength*. Within six months, Uber had $10 million in investments and never looked back. They succeeded in outsmarting an entire industry by creating a solution to what no one had really thought of as a problem.

The truth is, opportunity will seldom come knocking at your door. You're going to have to build the door first, create a path to the door, and make sure people notice.

Successful people don't count on luck. So, how do they create an opportunity and predict whether or not it will catch on? All entrepreneurs have several habits in common.

They pay attention. They notice what is happening around them. We experience annoyances every day, such as trying to hail a cab in the rain. A smart entrepreneur will consider this minor annoyance and think about how to solve it. They think about what people want and value, what could make life just a little bit easier. In effect, they go through their day asking themselves, "What if …."

When you start to ask, "What if?" you open your mind to all kinds of ideas. Uber is nothing but a car that picks you up. It's nothing new. But … "what if there were an app that could summon the ride in minutes, with all payment arrangements already in place …"

Another industry that is growing is food kits – meals delivered pre-chopped and ready to cook in 10 to 15 minutes. There's nothing new about food delivery. Supermarkets have been doing it for decades. But someone started to pay attention. The 1950s, when women happily shopped at the market and pridefully spent hours creating meals for the family no longer exist. Instead, women today are working long hours, are tired, don't always know how to cook, and the last thing they want to do is stop by the market, hassle through the checkout, go home and start cooking.

Obviously, someone thought … "What if … people could get pre-measured, pre-chopped fresh food delivered that would only take a few minutes to prepare?" While the supermarkets aren't overly worried yet, meal kit companies sold $1.5 billion in meals in 2016. So far, the market share is divided between half a dozen meal kit providers, but they are each concentrating on providing more value – vegan meals, organic meals and breakfast.

How has the meal kit industry caught on when supermarkets abound? The industry studied the potential consumer – young, busy, cooking-averse, interested in staying healthy, and – very important – used to having things done quickly. A generation that was born in the computer age is accustomed to instant gratification. Instant meals fit easily into the customer's lifestyle. Meal kit companies *created* a need and offered a solution.

To create opportunities where none exist, look around you. Make it a daily habit to ask yourself, "What if?" What could you do to make someone's life's better and easier? The answers to those questions has been the starting point of every successful entrepreneur. As we have seen, it doesn't have to be big or overly innovating. You merely need to predict what will add value to someone's life, and make it available. Find something that is missing, fill the void, and your competition won't stand a chance.

Watch for current trends. Meal kits would not be successful if it weren't for a younger, busier generations that is accustomed to quick solutions.

To outsmart the competition, develop the habits of:

1. Curiosity. Always looks at the world around you with a question mark. Allow yourself to become creative.
2. Determination. Persevere where others give up. Sometimes, it takes time and effort to predict what will work.
3. Healthy ego. When you believe in yourself, your skills and what is possible, you have what you need to create a new path. Remain optimistic, even if things look bad at the moment. You know that circumstances change, because you are the one changing them.
4. Commitment. Unless you are fully committed to what you are doing, your competition will move ahead.

Chapter 5: Know Your Customer

> Never interrupt your enemy when he is making a mistake.

The above quote isn't from Sun Tzu. It was said by Napoleon Bonaparte, but since he was another fierce warrior, we'll let its truth stand.

We've been discussing how to outsmart your competitor by giving customers extra value. But what if a company offers great value, is the only one offering it? What could possibly go wrong? Do you feel that there is no chance for you under these circumstances?

Remember the BlackBerry? Years before the ubiquitous iPhone, BlackBerry had everyone drooling. Everyone wanted one. The BlackBerry inspired passion in its users. When then-President Obama lauded his beloved BlackBerry, it became an instant status symbol. How do you overcome that kind of competitive advantage?

Does anyone use a Blackberry today? Probably not. Let's see how a company's refusal to even know who its customer-base was caused it to experience a huge fall from grace, and how smart competitors brought it to its knees.

BlackBerry was manufactured by RIM. It was the first phone with email capability, and an excellent product. It was a strong product, in great demand, and RIM should have kept improving the technology and made it even stronger. The company did not do that. Instead, they relegated the BlackBerry to a secondary role and concentrated on its Playbook. RIM ignored its own strength and focused on its weakness. The main problem was that no one could agree to whom to market this wonder-product. The CEO assumed corporations and government were the customer. Others in the company thought the BlackBerry should be marketed to individual consumers. With no one agreeing and no one in charge, nothing was done. RIM didn't even bother with market research. Incredible as it sounds, this popular product died of neglect.

Apple and Samsung swooped in with their iPhones and took over the market. Not necessarily with better products, but because they recognized a competitor's poor marketing style and a need to make the product available to a different market – the individual consumer.

Successful companies who can outsmart their competition know exactly who their customer base is. Their market analysis includes an in-depth profile of their potential consumers. This includes personal information such as age, education, hobbies and contact information. Their profile includes customers' likes and dislikes. This may sound intrusive, but the information is available, and smart marketers know how to use it. It's savvy to know what the consumer wants and to offer it. These days, it's a business necessity.

Companies who do not make these predictions will invariably end up losing instead of winning.

Take another company, Kodak. It doesn't get much more venerable than Kodak, the 125-year old manufacturer and seller of cameras, along with the necessary film. In the 1970s, a Kodak employee designed the first digital (non-film) camera. Management was less than enthusiastic and sat on the idea for almost 15 years when they should have been creating a need for digital cameras. In 1989, with a patent in hand, Kodak was finally beautifully positioned for another marketing slam-dunk when it introduced the first digital camera into the market. Never before could consumers get instant photos. How could Kodak lose with this?

Kodak lost because it didn't recognize their customer's demand for instant, digital pictures. Instead, they tried to protect their film business by pushing their film business and almost ignoring the new digital opportunities.

Do you think Kodak's situation is unusual? It actually isn't. The majority of companies are so set in their ways, they remain oblivious to what their customers need. A study revealed that 90 percent of companies don't bother finding out what the consumer really values. The assumption is that the customer is happy with what they are getting. If you don't listen to your customer, it is impossible to predict what products, improvements or services to create. Conducting simple surveys can reveal a lot of information that you can use to your advantage.

Chapter 6: Using Social Media to Outsmart Your Competition

It is a matter of life and death, a road either to safety or to ruin -Sun Tzu.

The old general is saying that you need to change when necessary when new tools present themselves. In a business war, social media is a valuable tool you cannot ignore. Everyone needs to use social media to their best advantage these days. With so much information out there, if you pay attention, you can predict the steps and plans of your competitor and outsmart him. Secrets are hard to keep in the rapidly-growing information age. As for you, be careful of the specifics you put out there into the universe. Your competition is watching you, as well.

Most businesses that use social media tend to pay attention to their own followers. They are, after all, their customer base. To outsmart your competition, you need to listen to your competition's followers, as well. After all, you want to turn them into your customers, right?

The importance of social media is in the numbers. You may be trying to build your own following, but you'll probably equal the 1.5 billion Facebook followers. These are people you need to reach.

Your competition has followers who might not be aware of you and what you have to offer. Perhaps some of them are old followers who have switched allegiance to your competitor. That is why you need to "listen" to and monitor who the competition is talking to.

Consider this. Every one of your competitor's followers is a prospective customer for you. They have shown an interest in the services or products provided by your competitor. If you have analyzed your own customer base, you know the demographics you should be engaging. They are your audience. You just have to reach him or her and transfer that interest to you. Engage these prospects by directly addressing them. Get them interested. You'll get a lot of information on how your competitor's followers think, and what they are looking for. This provides you with an excellent opportunity to get them to follow you. You should be providing content they will notice. Once you have their attention, you can create a campaign that answers the needs of your competitor's audience. Fishing in your competitor's pond is a very effective way to outwit your competitor on social media.

To show you how it can work, take a recent Twitter ad produced by a dating site. For weeks, the site featured the same nice looking, bald man. Just one Twitter user, perhaps sarcastically, tweeted. "What about someone with hair?" It could have been a joke, but starting the following day, that particular dating site and others suddenly featured men with an abundance of hair. Obviously, someone was paying attention. By listening to your competition's followers, it is easy to predict their needs and respond to them.

Get involved in social media discussions. They are open and available to all. You don't have to, and shouldn't be, selling anything at this point. The purpose is to position yourself as a player in the industry and to build a relationship. Let them know you have expertise that can help them. A bonus giveaway is a catchy move to attract someone without making an obvious sale.

Don't be afraid to engage your competitor with questions about his or her brand. If he or she doesn't respond, you can be assured other users will. Discuss your company with someone who seems dissatisfied.

Find ways to use relevant news headlines to promote your brand, even if the headline is unrelated to you. Disney did some major promotion of their princesses when Britain's Princess Charlotte was born. Dove used a hashtag, #beautyis, resulting in user selfies and responses and a better understanding of potential customers. These responses made it easy to predict what people were looking for in the general soap and beauty market.

An active social media presence enables you to create and maintain your brand's reputation as you emphasize the differences between you and your competitor. Respond to reviews, good or bad. This builds on your relationship and indicates that you are actively listening to and participating with your customers.

Seventy-five percent of buyers depend on and use social media before making a purchase.

That's a number you can't ignore if you want to succeed. Establishing your brand creates the kind of trust consumers want before spending their money. Your relationship with them should start *before* they buy. When they are ready, you are already a known entity, even if they've never been a customer. At this point, you can readily predict that they will be seeking *you* out before making a purchase.

Outsmart your competitor by targeting his or her Gmail ads. These ads are send to users who have indicated an interest in your competitor. Do a keyword check and target that specific email audience. That means when your competitor sends an email, your email will reach the same target audience. Sneaky, but very effective.

You can access and download Twitter users who follow your competition. This list can be used for targeting Twitter ads. This is an excellent way to directly focus advertising to people who've shown an interest in your competitor. They are already a likely market for your product. Use the ads to switch their interest from your competitor to you.

Facebook and Google offer superb opportunities to move ahead of your competitors for the simple reason, a lot of companies just can't be bothered. The problem is the same one we discussed in Chapter 1, the need to do an in-depth analysis of your competitor's company. This will take work, and most companies are focusing their efforts elsewhere, so if you do the necessary social media assessment, you will come out ahead by outworking and outsmarting them.

We've discussed the power of Facebook, with its billions of users. Everyone wants to get their ad in Facebook, and that's fine – for your competitor. You go the extra mile, because you goal is to outsmart that competitor. You need to make your ad attractive and enticing to lure the average clicker who is just looking. They may be vaguely considering making a purchase or opting for a service, but it's still a whim, a huge one maybe in their mind. Here's how to change that maybe into a yes.

Have an interest-provoking headline that begs to be clicked, such as, "The Secrets to Losing Weight No One Is Telling You." You can pretty much predict it'll get a click out of sheer curiosity. Arousing a prospective buyer's curiosity is a large part of the battle.

The next step is critical. Once the prospect clicks, what will he or she see that moves then to act – something like a $20.00 ebook on the topic they are interested in at no charge. Be prepared to make that offer of a free book. The odds are, he or she will take advantage of this and order it. Then, continue leading them through the landing page with requests of email address and/or phone number. Use this information to create contact information for further sales that are directly relevant to this consumer.

Create other enticing ads on Facebook that create an immediate need to act, such as a "Buy 2 get free shipping," "Sales end Friday," or

"Limited amount available." By predicting natural human behavior and reaction, you're creating an immediacy that your competitors offer of a $12.00 T-shirt simply cannot match.

Another mistake your competitor is likely to make is to target such a broad audience that it limits the ad's effectiveness. It amounts to a large ad budget for very little return. Facebook as an "Audience Insights" feature that lets you see which pages are of the greatest interest to your target customer by analyzing the amounts of "likes" the pages receive. This information is useful in creative target-specific content and ads.

Social media allows you to predict consumer behavior and provide an answer to their needs. This is a huge opportunity you should be utilizing immediately. Your competitor's customers are waiting for you.

Chapter 7: Use Guerilla Fighting Tactics to Outsmart Your Competition

If he is taking his ease, give him no rest- Sun Tzu.

If you have a thriving neighborhood business, you'll want that business to grow. Your target customer probably lives nearby, and your competition is down the block. You need to get the customer's attention before the other guy does. You've working on a smaller scale than some of the Goliaths, but you still need to grow your market share.

While a global social media audience probably won't help draw customers to your restaurant, hardware store or dry cleaners, a website will. If someone is looking for a specific service, you can predict they will pull out their smartphone or table to determine what is nearby.

The amount of shops without a website is surprising. It's almost as if they were doing business the same way their parents did. It's good to be known, and word of mouth advertising is certainly desirable. But, if someone is looking for, let's say, a nearby Mexican restaurant, and one has a website and the other doesn't, can you predict which one the customer will visit? Doing business without a website to give your customers relevant contact information simply no longer works in the digital age.

Every business, regardless of size, needs a website these days. It should describe the merchandise and services available and, obviously, stand apart from other stores. What does your business offer that the one a few blocks away does not? A good website is inexpensive, but will pay for itself in no time.

Besides creating a website, there are other strategies that will help call attention to your business. Use them, and watch your sales grow exponentially.

1. Print fliers and distribute them to offices, apartment buildings and stick them on cars.
2. Only a few small businesses use blog content to increase their sales. A blog is an invaluable tool to educate potential customers and stimulate their interest. If you own a hardware store, a blog with remodeling tips will attract attention.
3. You can have some fun with a false protest. Have a few employees carry signs that read, "Company A has the best sandwiches," or "Company B is fun to work for." You'll attract attention, smiles, and new customers who appreciate a sense of humor.
4. Leave business cards or fliers in other, unrelated stores. Advertise your bakery at the local yarn shop. Leave cards regarding your deli with the local insurance agent. Return the favor.
5. Offer demonstrations and freebies. Large markets can outsmart their competition

and gain customers by offering cooking classes. A sandwich shop advertised free sandwiches between noon and two o'clock on a particular day. Lines spanned 4 blocks for two hours. People love freebies, and the small investment can have huge returns. If possible, advertise your freebie on a local radio station.

6. Beside freebies, have giveaways. Calendars and pens with your name and phone number are a great way to keep your name in people's mind.
7. Sponsor a local school team and have T-shirts printed with the name of your business.
8. Find a partner with a related business. If you are an interior designer, partner with a local furniture store on both of your websites. This is win-win, as people looking for furniture will have the name of a decorator pop up, and people looking to redecorate will have quick access to new furniture.

9. Consider writing an editorial (or hire someone to write it for you) for your local paper that relates to your business. Your name and contact information will get circulated to all readers.
10. Leave coupons for discounts or free items in other local stores. This works especially well in beauty salons and restaurants. Get friendly with the staff (by offering them freebies), and they will hand out your coupons at the register.

Any of these tactics have predictable consequences. They are a call-to-action for potential customers who have your name handy when they need your services. Very few local businesses use these effective strategies, and the payoff can be quite big.

Chapter 8: Learn To Trust Your Instincts

We have discussed a number of strategies in how to become and remain successful and predict how to outwit the competition. These strategies work. An additional element, however, is intuition. Sometimes, the answers are clear. There will be instances when several choices are presented, and they all seem logical. How do you choose?

Every successful businessman learns to trust his instincts. There are times his or her inner voice screams to stop a project, even when all evidence points to the contrary. Other times your gut tells you something will work, even when your brain says no.

Your competitor probably is listening to all available information. You take the same data and do your own analysis, and then listen to your instincts. You know risks are necessary, and risks entail going with the unknown.

Being able to trust your instincts enough to take risks isn't fool-hearty. Instinct is developed over years with available facts. These facts may be deeply buried in your subconscious, but you know enough to respect them because innovation is frequently risky, but always rewarded. In order to predict success, sometimes you need to take the risks your competitor will not and go with your instinct. Let your competitor copy your innovation, but you will lead the way.

We've discussed the importance of listening, both to your competitor and your clients. You access your instinct by paying attention and listening to yourself. The information is there. You merely need to trust it. Asking yourself why something feels right or something else feels wrong is a good habit to get into on a daily basis. The unique ideas borne from such introspection is what enables you to move ahead of your competition.

To understand this, ask yourself why you want to be the best? What made you decide the entrepreneurial life was for you? It's doubtful that facts can answer those questions. The reasons are deep inside of you, on an emotional level. It was that intuition, combined with relevant facts that pushed you on your way. Emotions and facts are not natural enemies, but can work together to arrive at optimal results.

Before the men who started Uber had their facts, they were driven by their emotion: "Who wants to wait for cab in the rain?" Everything else came from that one bit of insight. If Walt Disney had thought only in a straight, linear way, we wouldn't have a silly mouse in polka dots pants ruling a major kingdom. Facts didn't support it, but Disney's instinct told him people would respond to the mouse.

If acting on instinct gets your nervous, it should. Because it's instinct, along with lots of facts, that are the winning combination that many people lack.

Following your instincts requires you to be flexible, which is another trait that every business leader must possess. The worse things anyone can say is, "It can't be done," or "It's never been done." People who ignore those negative ideas are the one solving problems and setting the rules for tomorrow.

Keep in mind that a strongly developed instinct can keep you from making huge, costly mistakes. You deal with people every day. How do you know whom you can trust, and whom you need to avoid? Trusting your gut when it comes to people you do business with can save you from potential setbacks; it can also move you forward when you know you can trust the individuals you work with.

In business, there is a lot of negative reaction when it comes to instinct. Business leaders like to think they are information-driven. Combining instinct with factual information can strengthen your position, especially if your competition is relying solely on known data.

Chapter 9: Find Your Niche Market

Rapidity is the essence of war: Take advantage of the enemy's unreadiness, make your way by unexpected routes, and attack unguarded spots.
– Sun Tzu

Let's assume you want to open your own business. Congratulations! You're on your way to successful entrepreneurship. Now, you're wondering, how can you stand out? You're thinking of opening a food store, car dealership, clothing shop ... there are lots of possibilities. Unfortunately, there are also a lot of other businesses that provide the same service and products.

All the rules of outsmarting your competition still apply, and you should adhere to them as you grow your business. Still, there is one more, very important thing you can do to shoot your business ahead of the rest.

You can create your own niche market.

What is a niche market? A niche is a specialization within a specific industry. It's being a specialist in a particular aspect of the business. Instead of offering more, you'll grow a larger business with less by narrowing your focus. This strategy is incredibly effective, especially in today's marketplace, where everyone is looking for something "special."

Instead of being a "generalist," a niche market goes after a more limited, but very specific target. Let's say you're ready to set up your own dental practice. You have your marketing plan all set out – internet advertising, fliers, etc. Still, there are lots of dentists. They all advertise as being "pain free." Why should a prospective patient choose you as they surf the internet looking for a dentist? What makes you stand out in this crowded, competitive field?

What do you think will happen if your tweak your plan and specialize as a dentist for children? You immediately establish a solid, viable market base, and more importantly, you stand out. When searching for a dentist for their children, you are immediately shortlisted among the general dentists. And growing your market share is much easier. You can visit schools and speak at PTA meetings about the importance of proper oral care – and, of course, hand out fliers and cards. You can leave literature at preschools and daycare. You're reaching parents who are looking for a children's dentist for the first time, and there you are, ready with all your information. Niche specialization sets you apart. Clients will automatically check you out instead of your "generalist" competitor.

Imagine you want to open your own car dealership. There are as many of those as there are dentists. They all proclaim low prices. How can you predict success in this kind of market? You can, if you specialize. Instead of just any cars, you can narrow your niche to sports cars, luxury cars, first-time car buyers, fleet vehicles, etc. By using your niche in print ads and internet ads, you've created your own customer base who will be seeking you out instead of the other way around.

If you're thinking of opening your own food store, you'll be facing fierce competition from supermarkets that are available on every other block. How do you convince customers to go out of their way and visit your store? You can offer specific ethnic foods, which can put you ahead of the game, but most supermarkets these days already have a good ethnic food selection.

What if you offer food items the supermarkets don't? A small food store in Chicago brilliantly specialized in foods that other supermarkets didn't carry – French Jambon, fresh sardines not in cans, but in barrels, pate de foie gras, and much more. Did they limit their customer base? Of course, but by doing so, they didn't just outsmart their competition, they made sure they had no competition for their merchandise. They were the only place in town where foodies could satisfy their cravings. They developed the largest market share in their category niche. In addition, they used superior marketing techniques. In the 1990s, there were import laws against importing Iberian ham, a special ham from Spain that famously is made from pigs fed on acorns. Months before the import ban was about to be lifted, articles started to appear in the Wednesday food section in the local paper describing this special ham, how it was made, how it could be used. The articles never mentioned the store. One Wednesday, however, an ad appeared in the food section: "Iberian Ham Has Arrived!" After whetting the public's appetite for months, the small store was the only place in town selling this rare ham. The lines of eager customers were out of the door.

Specialization is a sure way of knocking down the competition because it creates instant awareness. Any business can do it. If you're in advertising, specializing in a special field, such as insurance, you will attract more customers than a general advertising agency. A photographer specializing in children or weddings will readily attract customers in that niche market. A specialist is easier to find and saves the customer time. There is an air of exclusivity about the specialist. He or she is seen as an instant expert in the field, not just another business among many.

The greater the competition in a specific market, the greater the need for specialists will become. Their very uniqueness will draw customers away from competitors.

By being known as the niche provider, you can become the expert others seek. Write a small book explaining your field. A wedding photography can leave sample books in bridal shops. A pet store owner can specialize in great Danes or German Shepherds. An insurance agent specializing in first-time insurers can visit seminars for new home buyers, furniture stores, and mortgage companies. Speak at rotary luncheons. When you create your specialty niche, there are few limits to how you can grow, prosper, and leave the competition behind. Don't try to be everything to everyone. Be THE ONE to those who seek you out.

Chapter 10: How To Negotiate And Seal The Deal

Build your opponent a golden bridge to retreat across. – Sun Tzu

When you were younger, getting what you want was easy. You grabbed something and firmly proclaimed, "Mine!" With any luck, you'd actually get it.

That technique isn't going to work in business, when you want to seal a deal. Negotiating is an art, and to best your competition, you need to become an artist. Basic human nature can help you predict success. Your opponent wants something, and if they feel they are getting it, they will cooperate. The trick is to also get what *you* want. That's called win-win, and it's the best type of negotiating tactic for everyone involved.

Like everything else in your business, you start by being more prepared than anyone else. You can't seal a deal if you just go into a negotiation hoping for the best deal. You need to know what your opponent wants and needs and what motivates him or her. This type of knowledge helps you create the bridges necessary for the successful back and forth strategies of sealing a deal where you get what you want.

Start by asking for more than you expect. There's always the chance that you'll get it. More importantly, it offers you the opportunity to generously accept an opponent's lower offer (what you really wanted all along), while your opponent can feel he or she has won the round. Have an issue you are willing to concede. The opposition will think it has won and will be more open to conceding on an issue that is important to you. As stated above, it's all about win-win.

Whatever your opponent offers, don't accept the first number, even if the numbers are in your favor. If the initial offer is good, you will be able to get something even better. A simple, "That's not quite what I had in mind," followed by silence, will force your opponent to act. Avoid being too eager, even if you are.

Avoid hostility and arguments. No one benefits in a negative atmosphere. Always leave your opponent a graceful way out – a bridge to back away. You might be negotiation with him or her at some other point in time.

Be as open with your plans as you can be. This shows trust, which your opponent can match. Don't show all your cards, but allowing a peak at an ace in the hole can be beneficial. If you are unable or reluctant to reveal any business information, at least reveal some personal information, such as a hobby. Establish a relationship based on trust while you are negotiating. It creates a positive atmosphere. Keeping the mood light instead of tense will make your opponent more receptive to your requests.

Take your time when you respond. Either remain silent, and request more time. You want to avoid responding too quickly. A break in the negotiation indicates that you are not desperate. That's the image you want to present, even if you are anxious. Adhere to the old saying, "Never let them see you sweat."

Regardless of how the negotiation is going, have a bottom line in mind where you will walk away. Be firm on that in your own mind.

Keep in mind that a contract negotiation can entail more than price. Too many negotiators make the mistake of concentrating on money and nothing else. A smart negotiator knows to focus on other variables. Usually, there are a lot of options your competitor may overlook:

1. When you negotiate with a supplier, can you throw in free marketing advertising his or her merchandise for a better deal?
2. If you know your opponent is negotiating with you as well as your competitor, don't simply give in by offering a lower price. There are other factors you can point to, if you have done your homework. For example, point out that yes, your

competitor has a similar product, but he or she also has a history of late delivery and being out of stock. Never hesitate to attack your competitor's weaknesses.
3. Can you offer a better payment schedule than your competitor?
4. Can you commit to a larger order at a more flexible price?

Remember, even if you and your competitor are offering a similar product, a bit of creative negotiation can seal the deal for you.

Chapter 11: Be The Leader Who Comes Out Ahead

It is clear that there are actions you can take to create the kind of necessary circumstances that will allow you to win over your competitor. As you start your journey towards winning, you'll be surrounded by other people, especially your staff. You will need to inspire the same kind of passion and fire in them that fuels your actions.

Are some people simply born to lead? Perhaps some people have certain advantages, but leadership can be learned, and it's a skill that can be enhanced. The better you are at leadership, the more you will inspire your team.

You know you set the tone in your office. Make sure you encourage the type of behavior that will lead the team forward instead of backward. Make it clear that certain behavior is expected, and certain actions needs to be corrected.

Be willing to work with your team. Ask questions instead of merely spouting orders. Be honest when you have made a mistake. This will garner you the respect and loyalty you need to be successful.

Allow for open communication. If your team can't be honest about their fears or opinions, you will never have all the facts. Nor will you have their complete trust. Leadership based on fear and intimidation is doomed to fail and open the door for the competition to succeed.

Reward good performance and penalize bad work habits. People respond to positive reinforcement. If someone has worked hard, recognize the effort. If someone has let the team down, you must make your expectations clear.

Look to someone who has already achieved your dreams. A good leader knows there is always more to learn, and is eager to do so. Find a mentor who has done what you plan to do and watch him or her. Be open to new ways of doing things. Nothing strangles new ideas than an attitude of "I know what I'm doing and don't need more input."

Encourage your team to be creative. Make it clear that just because something has been done a certain way for years, it doesn't mean methods and procedures can't be changed. Welcome new ideas, even those that don't work out.

Being aware of what is happening is the best way to create your own opportunities. By being proactive and making things happen, you can easily predict the effect it will have on your competition.

Genuinely care about what you are doing. If you are not committed to your goal, your team certainly won't be.

Get to know your team. You're the boss, but you are also human. Ask how they are doing, what their interests are. The more you can show that you care about them, the more they will care about you. Learn compassion and empathy.

You will never move ahead of the competition without positive thinking. Encourage positivity within your team. If you truly believe a job can't be done, your team will pick up on the attitude and feel the same way. Don't belabor failures; instead, inspire a winning attitude.

Be aware of your own emotional state. Everyone has stressful days, but you can keep stress at a minimum. Avoid distractions, if possible. Meditation can be a great stress-reducer and keep your performance at top level.

Make creativity a habit. No matter how busy you are, sit back and consider how things can be done differently. Always keep an open mind. Be curious about everything.

Take care of yourself. Eat properly and get plenty of exercise. If you do not feel your best, you will be unable to give your best performance.

Learn to act instead of only reacting. Many people wait for a problem to occur before doing anything. Be proactive. Anticipate problems and act to prevent them instead of spending time solving them.

Good leadership is a winning mindset. Expect the best of yourself and your team, and you will get it.

Conclusion

In life and in business, you have competition. It's competition that drives you forward and brings out the best you can be. And to be the best, you need to outsmart your competitors.

You will be able to predict your competitor's moves and outsmart him by working harder and thinking differently. Understand the value of information. The more you know about any given situation, the more options you will have. Know you competitor, your customer, and the market. It's important that you understand your competition's weaknesses and use them to your own advantage. Make sure potential customers are aware of those weaknesses, as well as your own strengths. That's not rudeness; that's good business.

Most companies simply offer a product or service. Be the one that offers real value. By offering more or better than your competition, you will always remain a step ahead.

Look for opportunities for fill a need; if no such opportunity exists, create it. Opportunities abound, and they are all around you. Keep an open and curious mind at all times, and most importantly, keep asking yourself, "What if? That simple question will open the mind to ways to create and then fill a need that simple didn't exist before. By asking "What if," you will find answers to people's daily annoyances and provide the solutions. All while your competition is doing things the way it has always done.

We are living in an information age. Never before has there been so much information available to all. Used correctly, this information can help you predict what your competitor is doing, planning to do, and is unable to do. All you need to do is mine the data on Facebook, Twitter and other social media sites. Learn what people say about your competition and use that information to provide them with what they want. Directly interact with your competition's customers and provide reasons for them to choose you in the future. Offer them something your competition is not, including freebies that will pay for themselves. Consumers love a good deal, so it's up to you to convince them that that is what they will get when dealing with you.

While you are gathering information, this book will show you how to remain proactive and use offensive strategies to outmaneuver your opponent. Using offensive tactics opens up more and greater opportunities to get your message and your product to the attention of consumers. Most of these tactics are easy, but few businesses actually use them. That's what makes them so effective for you. These are winning and creative tactics that you do not want to miss.

If you are thinking about opening your own business, this book will show you the advantages of creating your own niche market. This is a market where you create your own customer base, and those customers will be seeking you out, instead of the other way around. Niche markets are a powerful tool to become the leader and expert in your particular field. Become a "specialist" and watch how quickly your market share will outgrow your competition.

The Art of Predicting consists mainly of being proactive so that you can be assured you offer a value that no one else is even thinking about. It's the best and more winning business strategy, so embrace it and make it yours.

Other books by Richard Carey on Kindle, paperback and audio

Pessimistic Persuasion 101: How to Talk Anyone out of Anything

www.ingramcontent.com/pod-product-compliance
Lightning Source LLC
Chambersburg PA
CBHW020455220526
45464CB00002B/991